BLACKMAN
THE FALL OF I

Take me back in time to where I was born
Free me from the enslavement I am now in
The joys of home cannot compare to any

At home I am free
Free to roam
Free to eat like I want and need to
Free to be me

Take me home to where I was born
Jamaica awaits me
Longville that is

Michelle Jean

Ah yes Blackman Redemption – the Fall of me Michelle Jean.

Wow because I truly don't know where to begin.

Let's start with the set up
My dream

Wow and I thought the set up was going to come from home – Jamaica but I know now that it will come from Canada.

The blue water is Canada but it matters not what they want to do with me or to me because the fall they want me to fall I will not fall.

I will not be the ploy for their plots
Schemes

Good God is on my side hence I know the goodness and greatness of him.

No matter what man do Good God can do better hence no matter what they try to do to me, they will not succeed.

They will fail because many nations – countries are slated to fall with Babylon – America.

Many will know what it's like to follow the devil. They will know what hell is truly all about.

Yes I am but one. A chosen of God – Good God and I must do that which he asks me to do despite my pain and hurt, my feelings of him.

It matters not the harshness of these words. The truth must come out and like I've said before, it is better to know the truth in the living rather than wait until you are dead because you will hear, "too late."

Like I've said, the lie did not work for Eve so how the hell do you expect the lie to work for you?

We can no longer live for death or as the dead; we must live for Life and have life.

Life is given hence we were born unto life and with life.

We are the ones to give up our lives for death.

We are the ones to believe that someone died for our sins when no one has died for it (our sins). No one can die for our sins.

When we do wrong do we not get punished? So tell me now, how can death save you if death is death – dead?

No one can take the place of your sins or for your sins. You are accountable for them because it is your name and your name alone that is on death's docket and I've told you this before.

No one can go to death and say, I will die in his or her steed – place because death cannot take that which is not given unto him – meaning written in his book.

If your name is not in death's book, death cannot take you and for someone to say they died for your sins is an infinite lie and an infinite sin.

Another person cannot die for your sins because Good God never told anyone to die for you or for your sins. Good God would never do this because Good God does not deal in death death does.

Death is the one to take you hence he's the one to deal in death.

True and good life cannot die. It can only grow up to see God – Good God.

Like I've said, life is a given. We are the ones to give it away to the wrong person and when things do not work out with you and them, you come crawling back to Good God.

Like I've said and will forever say. I don't care if you don't like me.

Frig I don't care if you want to set me up or want me to die. **_What I truly care about is your soul._** *You need to truly love you, hence you must do all the good that you can to go up and see Good God.*

Do not live to go down to hell. Live up to go see Good God.

Hell hath no water. It is pure atomic fire hence why live to want to go there?

If Good God is saying clean yourself up and come to me clean do it. Don't listen to someone that has not your best interest at heart.

Know that I infinitely and indefinitely do not want or need your soul. *My soul and spirit is secure with Good God despite my venting further on in this book.* **_Right now, I am in a dark space and place because darkness surrounds me and I have to get rid of the darkness. This darkness that I cannot see in so I truly don't need your soul or spirit. I cannot need your soul or spirit because I can't use it. And even if I could, I truly do not want or need it. What's yours is yours and you are to take good care of it._**

Do not give you away so freely.

Stop being a prostitute to sin because sin is not prostituting himself or herself for you. Sin is using you because the more people sin can get into hell the higher his rank above the demons of hell.

Demons go to and fro from the spiritual to the physical but sin cannot go to and fro. He was not ordained to do so hence Satan cannot walk to and fro on land.

He cannot walk to and fro in the spiritual either because he is not death. He is just a mere man that sinned. Now he's bound in hell. Yes she gave him life yet again but what life did she give him?

Death is the only one that can walk to and fro on land and in both realms (the physical and spiritual realm) hence some associate Satan with death and this is wrong.

We say Satan must deceive for a little while. Well let me tell you this, Satan has been doing that for more than a little while.

Satan has his agenda and his book which is the book of sin. The book of codes that was written to deceive you. And you have been deceived because everyone on the planet think the so – called holy bible was divinely inspired. Many of you live by this book without knowing that this book was written to bring you further into hell.

This book is Satan's book hence the book of sin. Satan is your god hence you worship him and praise him thinking you are worshiping and serving the true and living God – Good God.

Hence you marry by sin
Conceive in sin
Read the books of sin
Die in sin
Swear by sin
Live by sin

All that is sinful and unclean you do because Sin and Death is your god.

You do all for sin because your so – called divinely inspired book of filth is not of Good God nor is it inspired or divinely inspired by Good God.

Sinful and wicked men wrote it to deliver you unto death and they did just that. They delivered you right into the hands of death.

Now that Good God is talking you will refuse him and set me up to fall.

Well the truth cannot fall it can only rise.

I can only rise to see Good God but no evil or wicked and evil person can rise. All evil must go down to hell. This is why I tell you about the mountain of God – Good God. Not many people are on it and like I said, it's a shame because there are billions of people on earth.

Billions are going down to see sin and death and woo Nelly when you see them especially your sins.

Your sins are in hell waiting for you.
You will cry out.
You will burn.
You will die.

Yes the picture of hell was painted for you and everyone thinks that hell's fire looks like the sun. Well it does not. Hell's fire is the colour of an atom hence I call it atomic fire. This fire is infinitely hotter than the sun.

The rays or fire of the sun cannot destroy or burn the spirit but atomic fire can. This fire is the death of the spirit not the death of man or the death of flesh.

Your flesh is consumed by worms at death (physical death – the flesh) hence the spirit cannot die in the living – earth. The spirit can only die in the spirit, meaning after the shedding of the flesh.

No man, woman or child can give the command for the spirit to die.

The death of your spirit hath to do with your deeds hence good deeds are life eternal and bad deeds are death – your spiritual death.

Look at you and your sins. Hence no one can die to save you from them because your sins are recorded on your scroll – tree.

So Canada no matter how you try to set me up you will fail because Good God is not man. He is not wicked. He is good life and he is real.

You can do what you want to me but remember just as Babylon came a tumbling down you will tumble down with them. There fall will affect you and what will you do then?

How will your economy fair?
How will your people survive?

How will you feed and clothe them?

No one wants to hear the truth hence we live in lies and when things do not work out we cry.

We say we are sorry when it's too late.

Let me tell you this. I do not fear man or what they do because no man or woman including child can sacrifice my spirit or kill it. No one can kill the spirit hence there is hell.

You cannot live a dirty life and think you are going to get into heaven or Good God's abode in the end.

YOU ARE DIRTY. SO HOW DO YOU EXPECT TO GET IN?

No one can petition death for the next man either if Good God has not ordained you to do so.

Absolutely none!!!!!!

None of Good God's messengers can die to save you. We are to give truth – life. We cannot give death hence no one can die for you like I've said.

Life cannot kill life. This is the infinite truth.

DEATH TAKES LIFE – that which is given to him. And the way we do this is by the lies well tell and the sins that we do.

No man woman or child can escape this. No leader of a country can escape this. As leader, you pledge your allegiance to man and God to protect your people and when you send your people to war to fight and kill, then your broke the law – rule. (Thou shalt not kill). You must pay severely for this. Trust me your hell fire is not like the ordinary man because you committed a greater sin. You lied directly to God and man. You knowingly and willing did wrong hence the death of all your soldiers rests on you. When they (your soldiers) can escape death you cannot. You knowingly and willingly sent them (your soldiers) to take an innocent life – kill.

Yes innocent because that countries sins are not your sins. Those lives are innocent unto you because they had nothing to do with you.

You purposely sent your people to kill. Hence their sins INFINITELY AND INDEFINITELY FALLS ON YOU. *Their sins are recorded on your slate. So if your soldier had 2 years of sin and you had one, add his two years of sin on your plate plus whatever punishment – time sin and death tacks on for good measure in their court and courts of law.*

Wow. I so don't want to be some of you political leaders that say you run your country. Trust me death is going to run you with the fires of hell. If you can't dance now or here on earth you cannot dance in hell.

There will be no escaping hell for you. So keep thinking hell is not real.

Trust me real soon man – humanity will hear the dead cry on a grand – large scale.

All of you that say duppy don't walk will see them right in front of you. No scrap that because humanity is the living dead.

We do follow death. So our cries are death's cry – the cry of the dead – death.

Ah yes everything must change in time. Time is the master of all. Time has the key to death hence evil must die and will die shortly. Hence I worry not about what the devil and his children will do. Hell is there for them and in a little while they must come a tumbling down. Go straight to hell.

Michelle Jean

Oh God I want to get away
I want o run away from everything.

I need the out doors
I need nature
Sanity

God – Good God, I so do not know why you want
to keep me cooped up here?

I'm not a damned chicken
I am frustrated because nothing seems to be
working out for me.

I am bored
I truly love writing but now I am getting to loathe
the cold.

I can't take the cold nights
I can't take the loneliness
The emptiness

I can't move because of you.
It's like I am stuck here and I so want to defy
you.

It's like certain things you don't listen to me on
and I am fed up of it.

I can't take the pain of loneliness anymore.

I cannot take the restricted life anymore.

You're restricting me and I don't like it.

There are places – countries I so do not want to be in or go to so truly listen because you're not hearing me.

I need you to hear me.

I need you to feel my pain

I need you to know what I am going through.

Yes I rely on you for all.
Maybe I'm wrong.
But today, I truly do not want to be in this country. I truly need a vacation and you are truly holding me back. You are contributing to my loneliness – heartache. It's as if you want to control me – take away my life – freedom.

I don't like being controlled nor do I like being restricted, hence I truly want to leave you and do my own thing.

Michelle

Yes I'm hurt Good God
You continually hurt me by keeping me in a land I
so do not want to be in.

I truly love you, but why does my love have to
come at a cost to me and you?

Why does my love – true love have to hurt so
much?

Why does my love of truth have to hurt so much?

You want true love and thanks Good God but
when you get it you can't handle it.

I'm tired of complaining to you.
I'm fed up, but it seems as if you like it when I
beg you and complain to you.

You like it when we beg and grovel at your feet
like dogs begging at their master's feet.

This is wrong on your part hence we are not living
as your children on earth. We are living as dogs.
This is our life and reality and it cannot continue
to be this way. You cannot want to control in the
physical realm because no one can control you.
You don't like control, so you should not want or
need it for someone else.

God – Good God in truth, I truly cannot do this anymore.

I truly cannot walk in your hurt and pain.
I cannot walk in your lies.
I cannot walk in your time frame.

I have to be me
I have to truly love me
I have to be truly truthful to me.

I know it's different for you Good God but what about me?

Yes I'm spoilt but I truly need my life to be complete. And yes you complete me but today something is wrong. I saw the darkness around me and I truly do not want to walk in this darkness because in this darkness I have no sight. I cannot see.

I need to be truly happy with me and you.

I truly need to make me happy and I cannot sit around and wait until when you are ready.

Your time is not my time hence I have to do what's truly best for me. And because of this lack of unison in time we are not true to each other.

Remember you are further ahead in time.

Remember your time line is different.

Remember water time line is different and dry time line is different also.

Like I've said before. If you cannot make me truly happy then truly leave me alone. There is no reason or justification for us to be together. Truth and happiness means a lot to me and if you are not truly true to me, then it makes no sense for either one of us to be around each other. We must go our separate way in truth and honesty.

I do not want or need a yoyo relationship from you or with you. If I am your one and only let me be your one and only. Because I need to be truly happy with you and in you.

I truly need to be happy with me not just in thoughts of you, but in all the goodness that I do for me and you.

Michelle

I need to rest – sleep
I need to favour me

My body is stressed
Tired

I need to detox
Flush my internal organs - body

I need my spiritual power within to aide me.

I have to get in contact with my inner self – me.
I have to talk to the inner me but how do I get there?

How do I contact my inner self – being – Me?

What does my inner self even look like?

Many questions have I. No answers to get.

Michelle

Good God what a mess?

Mess, mess, mess

My daughter's room is a disaster area.

Like I've said, she needs to be on hoarders. She is that messy.

Gyal pickney can messy so?

She did clean the room but once again she tornadoed it.

God – Good God where have the cleanliness gone?

I so want to bolt faster than Usain Bolt, but where do I bolt to?

I keep complaining but I've yet to receive my plane ticket from you.

Wow. Good God, why can't you truly rescue me and send me on a good vacation where they cannot find me?

Michelle Jean

I am so not into the horseplay anymore Good God. I am so not in the mood.

Why am I losing the battle when it comes to my daughter and cleaning her room?

I am so tired of seeing the mess hence I have to kick her out real soon.

I want and need to see a clean place not a messy place everywhere and everyday.

My son's wall is a mess. It needs cleaning – wiping down and he refuse to clean it. Meaning he's lazy to clean it.

I truly can't take them – the nastiness.

The wall is dirty. Why the hell can't he clean it?

Why do I have to pick up and clean up after them?

I know, I know this is what we get for not asking you for good and clean children.

This is what we get for not marrying clean and good men.

We get nasty – messy children.

Yes we get children of sin because we did lay with wicked and sinful men including women.

I know we should not complain hence sin gives pain.

We live in pain
Marry in pain
And die in pain.

But God – Good God, I have to complain because I want and need to keep my place clean but is losing the battle with my messy children.

Michelle Jean
September 18, 2013

Yes Good God I have to complain
I have to complain to you about the nastiness of
my kids.

Good God, when do I stop complaining about
them and the messiness of them?

Wow.

Cleanliness passing the kids – children of this
world!

Good God, couldn't you have given us an undo
button?

No scrap that. Humans would use it to undo you.

Yes man would use it to undo each other. So
scrap the undo button, not a good thing.

God – Good God, couldn't you have made us. I
mean put cleanliness in our genes?

Wait a minute cleanliness is in the genes of good.
Whoever said humanity was good?

So scrap all Good God and let me truly start
again.

Michelle

It's a weird day Good God.

Too weird to be true.

Thank you for the laughter but where is my BBJ or Gulfstream 550?

Good God, you owe me because I truly need a vacation with you.

Good God hurry up. You are way too slow.

Why do you have to let me nag you so much?

Stop liking my nagging and let's go.

You know you are too slow and if I take you up, I will do something I might regret. So truly hurry up and deliver me your BBJ or Gulfstream 550.

I'm getting impatient Good God because I want to jet – fly away with you.

Michelle

Gooood where are you?

I need your BBJ

I need to jet away to someplace nice and warm.

Goooood where you at?
I can't see you. Where's your BBJ?

Gooood I am so going to bug and annoy you.

I want and need your BBJ.

You're too slow
Hurry up already.

*My good and true vacation is calling me and you
are keeping me cooped up – tied up in the cold.*

Goooood you're suppose to truly love me.

*Yes I went there. I need our/your BBJ. I need to
fly away to someplace nice and warm.*

I need to enjoy life and not be so bored.

You know you're boring.

Don't you dare say it because I know I'm boring.

Goooood – Good God where's your BBJ?

I am so not going to stop nagging you until I get your BBJ to fly away.

I don't care if you get pissed off at me. I want your good BBJ or Gulfstream 550.

Not tomorrow.
Not a year from now, but today.

Right now.

Goooood – Good God, where's your BBJ or Gulfstream 550?

I need it right now.
Did you lend it out?

No. So where is it? Your BBJ or Gulfstream 550?

Yes I'm annoying you because I truly need your BBJ – good airplane.

Michelle J.

Goooood – Good God, I am going to throw a tantrum.

I am going to be worse than a spoilt brat.

Where is your BBJ?

Stop hiding it from me.
Stop keeping me waiting.

Where is your BBJ?

I know it's not in the shop.
I know it does not need repairs or maintenance, so where is it? Where is your BBJ?

Stop hiding it Good God.
Hear me and give me your BBJ.

And no I do not want or need to fly solo. You have to be there with me at all times. You have to be my pilot and co-pilot at all times.

Yes I'm demanding but that's me.

We have land and lands to clean. Economies to stabilize.

People's lives to fill with joy and I cannot get around on a commercial airline. I need your Good

BBJ or Gulfstream 550 to get from point A to point B.

I need you in all that I do.

I know you are tired but we need a BBJ or Gulfstream 550 to get around.

We can have a bed on the BBJ.

You can sleep while I write and play. And yes sometimes truly bug you as I am in awe at the clouds. Yes the cloud formation is beautiful. What a beauty you created in the sky.

So God – Good God truly hurry up with our good and new BBJ or Gulfstream 550.

If you do not have one readily available, place a special order for me and you so we can jet – fly away real soon.

Michelle
September 18, 2013

Ah Good God I need you.

I truly need a vacation.

I'm getting miserable yet again.

I know the reason for my misery hence I am truly bugging you for a good vacation.

Good God open up your doors to me and truly help me to get a vacation right now if not real soon.

Good God, I see the undesirables so truly please send them back.

I truly need a good man.
A giver not a taker.

You are dear to me Good God so I truly refuse this taker. So please do not send him back to me.

I know who I want and need Good God and it is not him. So please do not send him to test my waters, because this man I infinitely truly refuse. I truly do not want him so no more testing please.

Michelle and Michelle Jean

I feel like a failure
No not a failure

I'm just not happy in mood.
I feel caged
Stuck
Confused.

Confused as to why I am in a land that I don't want
to be in.

Confused as to why I have to be here – cannot
move.

I want to pack it in.
I want to escape the cold
Want to leave this country.

My feet are tied
I cannot leave here
I cannot be free because God – Good God won't let
me.

Why am I caged God – Good God?
Why am I caged?
I want to be free
Free to roam and be happy.

I want to be free but God – Good God won't let me.

Michelle Jean

My world is not my own because I am not free.

My world does not belong to me because my spirit and flesh is jailed in a land it does not want to be in.

My world is dark because I cannot see the light.

I cannot see in pure darkness but yet I have my guide.

*The sea is there
But darkness is all around me.*

I have the single key but where can it take me – lead me? What door or doors can I open with it?

I have hope but where is God – Good God in all of this?

*I am in the dark.
I have to find the light.
Climb that mountain in order for me to be okay.*

I see the mountain but I have to come out of the darkness to get there.

If I do not climb the Blue Mountain my life will not be okay.

I need it to be.

I truly need to be free.
Truly need to get to Blue Mountain even if it's only for one day.

I have to get there even if it's for a day or two.

I truly need to find me – be on that mountain alone.

I need to find heaven
Paradise
Good God's abode.

I need to be free.
Because darkness is all around me.

Darkness consume me and I have to find the light.

My true light
The light of God – Good God, my true me.

Michelle

Free me from the enslavement of this darkness that surrounds me Good God.

*Free me from the chains that bind and bound me
Hold me*

*Free me from the dungeons of hell
The place that I truly do not want or need to be in.*

*I am but woman
Your child but my way is unclear.*

I want and need to be with you but where? It's unclear.

*I need clarity
I need hope
I need you to truly be my faith, hope*

*I need you to be truly truthful and honest to me
I need the lies to stop between me and you
I need you to be constantly there for me.*

Free me now Good God and let me be on your good and true mountain.

*Truly let me find you.
Let me find self.
Let me be free from all sin – sickness of man – humanity.*

Free me now Good God.
Truly free me.

I need to be on your mountain – Blue Mountain.

I need you Good God. Please help me. I cannot go home because the land and people are dirty – unclean.

I am in the dark when I am in Jamaica in the spirit.

I do not want to drive or walk in the darkness in Jamaica. I need to be in the light at all times.

Yes the Babylonians have all the jobs in Jamaica but Good God what is to be must be.

My own people sold you out this is my reality.

I cannot change what's been done. I can only change me for the better.

Too much darkness surround me Good God, hence I cannot truly see in this darkness. I have to feel in this darkness with that one single key. I have to arrive alone but yet I do not walk alone.

Michelle Jean

God it's September 19, 2013 and I am pissed.
Royally pisssed, hence I will swear in this book.

I have a last child that I wish I had an undo button for.

What possessed me to have him?
It's a constant struggle trying to raise him during the school months.

My stress level is up there because of three of my children and right now I truly want to run away.

I need to run away less I die.

I don't want to explode because if I do the cops will come. I would truly take out all my frustrations on them and right now the explosion is massive.

So it's better to walk away than to truly massacre them with my frustrations and anger.

From mi bane mi neva si pickney so.
Lazy
Stinking attitude
*F***ing nasty.*

Nastier than sin to raas.
Stupid and ambitionless because education a pass dem.

*It's like these f***ing black kids are our failure.*
Dem no want education
Dem no want good talking
Dem no want good telling
A good home.

They don't want a good future for themselves.
Instead of staying in school and further yourself,
dem stop an a go do drugs – weed. Pan top a dat
*dem f***ing lie an alcoholic.*

Mi haffi buss mi ass off fi dem and ambition pass
dem.

That's why if I could leave everything that is good
and true to my first child trust me Good God, I
would because he more than truly deserves it.

The rest, F them because I am truly getting to
dislike them due to or because of lack of ambition,
nastiness and dirty attitude.

Michelle Jean

No Good God, I can't blame you anymore for having them because not even hog want them to the hell I have to go through in raising them.

It's beyond me why these kids cannot change their dirty attitude and ways.

As a parent, you bust your ass off in raising them and instead of making you raise your head up high, they make you hold it down in shame and disgrace.

You are stressed out and they add more to your stress.

Dem no du nothing apart from hang out with the wrong crowd, keep their room and walls dirty and I am truly fed up of this because talking have no use to them. I am all talked out.

Dem not even wash dishes or clean the bathroom.

Garbage pile up and you have to argue with them just to take it out.

Yu haffi cuss dem fi bathe.
Yu haffi cuss dem fi du homework.
Some don't even read a book and I have so much but yet dem complain fi food.

Why the hell should I feed or even clothe them?

They don't mop the floor.

I have to pick up after them like I am their damned maid – servant.

Dirty clothes, dirty clothes, dirty clothes everywhere.

They don't sweep the floor.
Laundry some don't even do.

My first son; Good God truly thank you for him because if it wasn't for him I would be dead already.

You truly sent him – gave him to me and I truly, infinitely truly thank you for him. So truly bless him with all your goodness and truth Good God. Truly thank you because you did do good and true by me by giving me him.

Michelle and Michelle Jean.

No Good God I am truly sick and tired of my children from 2-4.

The second one because he's ambitionless when it comes to friends and my life. I truly cannot trust him when it comes to friends and my life and that is sad.

When it comes to money, my money I can trust him.

Taking care of me I can infinitely trust him. But when it comes to the friends he keeps, I truly cannot trust him. I truly do not like some of his friends because ambition is not there when it comes to them achieving something in life. Furthering their education. And I feel sorry for none. Only a couple I like because they are furthering their education to better themselves later on in life. They have good life choices.

Yes we all make bad choices but from slavery until now we have been making bad choices and can't stop.

We all know about slavery but instead of holding our heads up and say no more, we continue to hold our heads down and hang on to the slavery bullshit anthem.

Instead of gravitating to good, we gravitate to evil – bad things.

We've adopted the nasty and stinking ways of the Babylonians and now look at us. ***Bob Marley told us everything we need to know about the Babylonians and we refuse to listen to his teachings.***

He warned us about them. Even told us that you Good God would never give them power over us but yet we can't listen. We go so far as put their stinking almshouse hair in our heads and call it weave. That's how nasty and disgusting we've become. Our own hair we don't want.

We've even adopted their stinking culture by putting filthy henna on our bodies.

We wear their nasty clothes and even marry them and think we are doing something good.

Look at it Good God, from Eve's generation until now we have disgraced and shamed you to the max and cannot stop.

We fight and kill each other for stinking Babylonian idols and books. Then turn around and trample you down for them.

When do we wake up and stop Good God.

Yes I am on a racist rant because no one can see the truth.

No one wants the truth. We all want lies.

Babylon has and have been using us as their scapegoat every since time. Meaning for almost 24 000 years and we still can't learn.

The book of Genesis is their true beginning meaning the death of Abel was to be the death of the black race. They were to kill us and they are doing it hence the blood sacrifice of Abel unto death – sin, who is Melchesidec otherwise known as the angel Michael – the angel of death.

He is the Hebrew Mutuyahu (the god of death) that humanity knows nothing about.

Truly look at us Good God because we've become graduates of their murderous and thieving systems.

Instead of learning, we choose to wallow in their filth with them. Hence Eve (Evening) had pain. Gave birth to children in pain.

It meant we were to feel the pain of raising our disobedient children in pain and alone.

We gave birth to pain – our children.

It also meant men – the fathers of these children would abandon us like you did Good God. I know you didn't leave us we left you because we chose sin – death over you. But there is no difference in my book. We do not have you because we are no longer clean.

We are dirty and you cannot reside with us in our dirty homes.

Good God, look how hard we try as single parents and it's our children to break us – let us hold our heads down in shame.

Instead of helping us to rise they help us down to hell.

I guess God – Good God we are no different when it comes to you because we are the ones to let you hold your head down in shame and disgrace on a daily basis because of our sins our untruth.

Michelle Jean

I am in a daze, muscles about to give way.

No strength in my body.

What is the normal with me?
What is the normal in my life?

I see the mountain but darkness surrounds me.
Yes I am being guided out of the darkness but what's up with the big ripe oranges?

Though I did not pick them up, I am truly beginning to hate fruit dreams.

They are a hindrance for me hence they mean nothing to me anymore.

Fruits are not my goodness hence they do not pertain to me.

Lately I've been seeing all types of fruits but yet, these fruits are not clean on the inside.

They are rotten hence old people sey, if yu no mash ants you cannot see what's inside of their bellies. Hence, these fruits to me are dirty and unclean people.

These fruits are pretty on the outside but filthy on the inside.

But what I so do not comprehend, is how the blue – dark blue sea correlates to all of this?

I am seeing more dark blue seas hence I do not know what the blue seas represent.

Strange – weird but I cannot let these things bother me.

I've mashed a lot of ants with these books and it's infinitely and indefinitely forever ever going to stay this way.

The truth needs to be told despite the heartache and pain. The pain that will now reach me.

I have to be me despite the set up for me to fall hence the name of this book.

I have to stay firm and true to the truth. Everyone wants to hear lies and when the truth comes they reject it. Well no more because like I've said in my other books, the devil's reign is up. Sin had his say and now Good God is talking.

Hell is real and no one is going to go into hell and save anyone because hell is that dirty. Hath fire. And clean cannot mix with unclean. Psalms One

Michelle Jean
September 19, 2013

I do not have a last stand.
I do not have a choice.
I have to do what I need to do.

I have to live a life of truth despite my views.

Life we say is not fair but life is what we make it.
Life is what we live and we have to live it true –
good and clean.

Yes my feet are tied and I am angry. It's as if something – someone does not want me to leave here – leave Canada. As if I am bound here.

I don't know, but this spiritual hold, I have to break because it is so annoying.

Why are my feet bound?
Why can't I go to and fro like everybody else?

Why do I have to be restricted to just this one land – place?

It's like a noose is around my feet. Whenever I make a turn to go here I cannot do it. I am being held back. I want to flee and be free but I can't.

I want to be free but it feels like I am dead.

Dying a slow death.
Freedom I cry, but no freedom is there.

God – Good God is keeping me bound in jail and I am so getting pissed off at him.

I want to bolt – flee to another world – land. Another universe so that God – Good God can't ever find me.

Stress, stress, stress
I want to flee (Jonah)
Truly need to be me.

Freedom I cry, but there's no freedom there.
Bound am I, can't get loose.
Failure's I've had
A few

Freedom I need
Truly unbound me
Let me flee and be free

Freedom, freedom where are you?
Truly where are you?

Release me and truly let me be free.

Michelle Jean
September 19, 2013

My life is so not my own and I am fed up of it.

The traffic of the in and out business is getting to me and I so cannot handle it.

There's no rest for me because of my children's friend.

I cannot take the noise
I cannot take the stress

My body failing and I am fucking tired of the traffic jam in my house.

I do not know how some parents do it, but I so can't.

My weekends are to be free and that cannot be. Oooh I'm ready to scream because it's not just humans, its dogs too.

I am so fed up that I want to disobey God – Good God and go home to my dirty home – Jamaica.

Right now I could not care less if the country is dirty. As long as I get away from my children and the traffic jam that's in my house.

I so want and need to be free that I cannot let God – Good God stop me from doing what I want and need to do.

I need peace and tranquility and I cannot have it in my home.

I don't fucking care if I explode like a fucking volcano so long as I explode.

I am so fucking tired of this stinking gutta belly almshouse life I am living with my children. It is truly getting to me hence I have to vent in the wickedest of ways.

Today I want and need my children to be gone so that I can live a clean and peaceful life without them and their traffic jams – friends.

Michelle
September 21, 2013

I can't sleep because of my kids.
I can't have a good life because of them and the fucking noise at my head.

They are so getting to me.
They are so fucking lazy (except for one) but yet I have to do all for them.

Fuck, I am ready to walk out of their fucking lives and never fucking return.

I truly don't give a fuck if I become unclean in the eyes of God – Good God because I am fucking fed up of my kids and the life I am living (in).

It's after 1am Sunday morning and I wish I was a fucking drunk that partied hard and don't have a fucking care just to drown them out of my thoughts – head.

No. I am at that crossroad where I don't want my children around me anymore. Sad but it's true because I'm going through too much. The fucking nastiness is getting to me and no matter how I talk they do nothing – nothing gets done.

So yes, I want to fucking leave because being a single parent and a nice person is fucked up. Being a single parent and a nice person means shit in this forsaken world, because no matter how hard you try with your children, you get fucking nowhere. It's like they don't fucking care.

The little things to help you, they don't want to do, but yet you have to provide all for them. Fuck single parenthood.

Fuck those fucking sperm donors that leave you to raise their children all alone.

Fuck them, fuck them and fuck the stupid judicial system too. Fuck them all because if I was a judge, I would fucking make these stinking gutta belly drangcrow dem stan up and be a father and mother to their children.

Why the fuck should one parent do it all alone?

Why should one parent bare the burden of raising children alone? It wasn't her alone that fucked and get them. You had a part in this scumbag, so look after your fucking children with me.

Yes I'm fucking bent hence I get down on my children. One parent can't do it all. She or He will get stressed – burnt out. Come on now.

Yes I need a fucking vacation and I can't go to the fucking land of my choice because it's fucking unclean and I am restricted from going there. But today, to the way I feel fuck everything.

Fuck restrictions
Fuck obedience
Fuck everything

I am not a fucking caged animal.

I feel fucking caged by God – Good God and who the fuck wants that?

Fuck everything this morning. Even fuck God – Good God because I am limited. Fucking limited in life and I fucking hate limits – restrictions. I need freedom not restrictions. I cannot walk because my fucking feet are tied because of him and by him.

Yes I am venting and who the fuck cares. No one knows what the fuck I am talking about when I say my fucking feet are tied. No one knows about fucking spiritual ties. You are bound, caged like a fucking animal. You cannot move. You are bound and there isn't a fucking thing you can do about it to get loose.

So this morning fuck everything. This is my way of letting off my steam.

Michelle and Michelle Jean
September 22, 2013

Yes I am venting and I do don't care if I piss off God – Good God because I am being restricted in life and my feet are tied.

Who the fuck wants to live a restricted life with a god that don't even care?

My feet are literally bound – tied. I know they are because I can feel them. I know the tie and this is a spiritual tie.

This tie I cannot break no matter how hard I try.

When God – Good God restrict you, you cannot move. Go anywhere hence I want so much to disobey today. I want to be like Eve – Evening and disobey.

People it's hard not being able to move.

People do you know tied?
I am mentally tied
Physically tied
Spiritually tied

You know when you want to escape your dungeon but can't?

I am so locked away and it feels like I am in a prison. I cannot move because I am caged. And yes I fully comprehend and overstand why so many before me fail God – Good God.

The road is hard to walk – travel because you are the only one on this road. There is no one to meet because there is no one to meet.

It's like you're going mentally insane at times.

You have no one to reach out to and celibacy is fucked.

You need intimacy and can't have it because no one is the right one in the eyes of God – Good God, so you have to go it alone.

Waiting is a fucking sin because waiting is fucked. Plays havoc on your psyche.

No wonder many of us go fucking insane because the road we have to travel is a fucking sin. Fucking lonely and trust me meditating on God – Good God does not fucking help. It just brings you further and further into depression because you do get fucking lonelier.

Michelle
September 22, 2013

My life is crap right now because there is no peace in my life just pure noise.

It's after 1am and TV is going.
Kids are loud and I cannot take it anymore.

Weekends are to be relaxing time and I can't have that because of my fucking pickney dem.

A fucking mama alone and I am being stressed out to the max.

It's a fucking pity there was undo button that I can use to send them the fuck back up the birth canal.

The undue stress
The undue pain
The heartache hence woman were to have children in pain; the pain of raising them.

Michelle Jean
September 22, 2013

A vacation would do me good right now. I don't care where, just as long as I piss of God – Good God and stick it to him for not sending me on a good and proper vacation.

Look how long I've been yearning to go on vacation and cannot go.

I truly need a vacation away from the noise of my children and their friends. I need time away from the game playing and the noise of the TV.

Trust me I fucking hate TV hence I do not watch television.

Nothing on TV interests me. News, I glance through the internet barely and it is becoming rarely now.

Television is a hot mess hence I care not for the fucking messes of the world. So long as it does not affect me and my life who the fuck cares? I have my writings and that's the way I need it to be.

Michelle Jean
September 22, 2013

Yes it's my venting day and I so don't care who don't like it.

Walk a mile in my fucking shoes if you think you can. I relish peace and quiet and I literally hate noise.

Noise should be banned in the home and outside after a certain time. Yes preferably after 9:30pm.

No one should drive.
No TV should be played.
No music allowed.

Well we'll keep the good soul music like cry for you by Jodeci, unconditional love Jah Cure, Romain Virgo's can't sleep and I want to go home.

Good singer. I truly love him but waaaaaay too young for me. Not into the so so young boys – young men but if I was, he's one of them that I would snag for real.

Oh lord have mercy. Wow. African music here I come because I was listening to some South Sudanese music and I am inlove.

People pretty skin dey.

Truss mi. Sudanese skin more than black and pretty.

Wow.

People you have not seen black and beautiful until you've seen Sudanese black skin.

Trust me, if I could bottle their colour – beauty and nyam it (laugh) I would.

People I am inlove with their complexion. I could sit all day and go wow. This is perfection. Lord have mercy because Good God knew black beauty.

What a people dem skin dark and pretty. Trust me I can look at them – their skin all day without getting tired.

Black people unnu skin no pretty like Sudanese black; true Negro – Niger people. Yes the water or river people.

Good God truly did me proud when he made – gave Sudanese people true beauty. Black Beauty.

Michelle
September 22, 2013

Yes I am still mad but the vicious venting is somewhat over.

I know some of you are saying wow she's gone. She needs a shrink. But you would be too if you are being restricted.

My road is lonely because Good God never called me and someone else, he called me alone.

Frustration do come in or set in because you want to vacation here (in your homeland) and you cannot.

There are so many things you want to do but cannot. If it's there's this wall before you and everywhere you turn – try to go, that wall is right there with you and it is getting frustrating. Hence I vent on Good God because if I go to man they are going to say, I am disrespectful. I need to release my anger and writing is my only outlet hence I vent on God – Good God. I know he comprehends as well as overstand and understand. I am alone on this road and I don't want to be alone anymore. I cannot come off because I am on the road of truth.

Yes, I know God – Good God is there with me in this storm but it's hard. I want and need the storm to be over when it comes to me but it cannot be. So long as I am in a world filled with wicked and evil people the storm will always be there.

I want to live but yet cannot live.
I want to sleep but can't sleep.

I don't know if anyone of you have or has ever felt tied. Like you want to move but can't. It's like cement blocks are holding you back – down. No not cement blocks. Cement blocks cannot describe what I am talking about. Hence cement blocks are the wrong description.

It's more like impenetrable walls surrounding me. You can't go around them or go over them.

It's like you cannot move and you want to defy everything including God – Good God because you don't feel your feet should be tied.

It's like everyone around you can move freely but you can't and it angers me.

It's like you can't reach out and text someone and say meet me at Country Style, Coffee Time or Tim Horton's for a coffee or tea.

It's not like you can rent out a club for you and family and just go dancing, you and your family.

It's not like you can call someone and tell them how you feel. Trust me none will understand so you have to take out your frustrations and pain out of God – Good God just to get that spiritual release that you need.

This frustration is not once in awhile. It's a lot of times, hence I tell you, I know why some messengers fail. The road is hard when you are on it alone. You have no support and it seems like you have no support from Good God either. You have to go through this faze.

It's not like I can text someone all night just to keep me or each other's company when I can't sleep – he or she can't sleep.

Yes there are days when my phone shouldn't ring. Hence home phones – at least my home phone is for emergencies or important calls. Other than that, don't bleeping call me to gossip. No I don't want to know who is breaking up with whom. I have sight because I know long before some of you with some people. And yes I have TMZ, E News, Lainey, Celebritchy and Blossip, you name it, I have them just for that.

Wait, wait no one calls my phone to gossip. Yeah me!

Michelle Jean September 22, 2013

Ah yes what a life?
The noise of the inside has died down.

Refrigerator running – noisy!
The occasional car driving by. Now noise in the hallway.

I need peace and serenity.
Damn I need to get laid.

Yes I said it. This bleeping celibate life is getting to me.

My body is dry
Running on empty hence to a large extent the misery.

Fill up my tank and let me be young again. Damn I need someone to truly oil my cherry tree.

No for real. How does some people do it? Damn it's going on seven full years.

No wonder I am old and miserable because the body needs fuel – sexual fuel.

Yes your body do need sex. But hey when you are not getting it you are miserable as hell. You become truly miserable like me. No, I am not insane yet and I cannot go out there and pick up any – a good ass ride. Shit, even if I could, I couldn't.

I'm like an aggressive pit-bull.
Miserable in looks and stance.

Damn I'm like an every one repellant. Hence men are so not drawn or attracted to me.

Weird because if I could attract good and true men and women I so would attract them all.

But NOOOOOOOOOOOOOO!!! I have to be the repelling one like a frigging skunk.

Damn it would be nice if I could break the barrier down.

Some women have no problem attracting the handsome ones. Me, hell no, I can't even find one.

Yes there are many a honey out there but for me, a honey isn't a honey if he doesn't have the right look – the right and good everything. That which is goodness and truth, both external and internal. He must have fidelity meaning he can never ever cheat.

Michelle and Michelle Jean
September 22, 2013

Yes it's Sunday morning and I so cannot sleep.
Time for a change. I am so going on vacation.

No, I don't need an oil change before I go.

Do not need a young stud to pick my cherry tree.

Do not need a boy toy to bore me.

Need paper and pen
Pencil' and erasers
Sharpeners and a trusted lap top.

I need a hotel far away from the noise.

Need to enjoy the night air and the night breeze.

I need to get away hence I want and need to piss off God – Good God because he did not send me his BBJ or Gulfstream 550 so that we can jet away.

Yes, I want to truly piss off God – Good God because he sees my need for a vacation and he refuses to help me.

Instead he's keeping me here. Does not want me to go anywhere.

Now I am going to piss off God – Good God for tying my feet.

I am going to defy him just because I am spoilt. Well I truly need a vacation.

I am so tired of begging him for one hence I am so going to piss him off until I get one.

I am going to go home to my dirty land just to piss him off.

<u>No wait, I can't do that because that would truly hurt him. Got to piss him off some other way then.</u>

Yes I want to piss off God – Good God because I truly need a vacation.

Don't know how yet, but I will find away. Yes I need his BBJ or Gulfstream 550 so I can jet away. Fly to South Africa or maybe somewhere on the continent of Africa but truly not Ethiopia, maybe, just maybe Mali.

Michelle Jean
September 22, 2013

Kenya open your doors to me.
Congo, Nigeria, Niger, Zimbabwe
No not Eretria or Somalia
Maybe Lebanon, wait no.

Libya, Morocco, Tangiers, Tunisia
All the black lands of Africa

No, not Reunion

Yes to Ghana, Swaziland, Lesotho, South Africa

Ah Mother Africa
The birthplace of life
Freedom and slavery

Out of many we came. We are one people that were true to life.

Yes we gave up life hence the womb of Africa cries out to her people, his people, help me.

The womb cry out and ask where has her good black people gone?

We were the original creation, the originators hence Africa, the Motherland, our true ship home.

We are Nubians. The true children of God – Good God. We are good and true. We just lost our way and way home.

We build
We fought but the fight is no more.

War – death is not the answer.
Only truth – that which is our destiny.

Africa – Mama Africa
The giver of life
The birthplace of life – true life

Africa – Mama Africa
The womb. I so want to come home and be with you.

Africa – Mama Africa
I am calling out to you
Hear me now
Receive me
I so want to come home even if it's for a week or two.

Africa – Mama Africa
I'm calling out to you
Please receive me
I truly need you
I truly need to come home.

Michelle and Michelle Jean
September 22, 2013

Ah it's sleepy time and I so cannot sleep.

I so cannot go back to sleep because I am not tired.

Need to tire out my body.

It's after two, maybe three in the morning and I so cannot sleep.

Can't bug anyone not even God – Good God if I wanted to.

The venting is over.

Need to get me some sleep but can't because I am so not tired.

Don't want to listen to music just want to tire my body out so that I can get some sleep.

Man if I could write music I would.

Don't even want to put any romance novels on paper.

My days for those are done it seems. As of late all I've been doing is writing books in the Michelle Jean line of books. I so want and need to design some clothes.

No it will not be a yearly thing. The clothing line will be so very often.

Me. I need comfort; to be comfortable in my own skin. And the less clothing the better. Meaning people should feel comfortable in what they wear.

We should dress for self and not others.

We should be happy with who we are.

We should truly love self and do for self. Hence we are to make ourselves happy.

Yes, I so want and need to do so many things but the cooped up and pent up life is so not happening.

Yes, I want to be free and it's time I break the reigns or hold of God – Good God so that I can be free in me.

Michelle and Michelle Jean
September 22, 2013

It's weird but if Good God truly wanted us to succeed in life, would he not make our journey easy and not so sickly?

It's amazing how you tell God – Good God you are lonely and you feel caged and he has done absolutely nothing to truly help you curve your loneliness. Yes I am happy with him in many ways but the loneliness of walking alone and doing things alone is getting to me. He God – Good God is not human and being human you need to be truly loved by someone. There are things Good God cannot give you on a physical level. **<u>This is the reality of my life hence I am truly lonely at times.</u>** *I cannot talk to the walls and the people that you talk to sometimes do not comprehend or overstand what you are going through. It's not like you can go out there and make friends. You are prevented from this hence you are alienated from unclean people.*

The road is so damned hard because you have to walk alone. It's a wonder why the failure rate with God – Good God is so high and the success rate with sin is so astronomical.

I do not understand or overstand why life with God – Good God have to be so hard.

Like I said, it's as if God – Good God wants you to fail.

Loneliness sets in
Yearning sets in and it's as if you are caged.
Can't do a damned thing.

You accept goodness, good life but what good are you doing for self when you have to walk alone?

What good are you doing for self when you are lonely?

The road to God – Good God is painful and depressing. No wonder we fail because we are like caged animals – controlled.

With God there are many places you cannot walk. You cannot walk amongst the wicked and the unclean.

Oh well, that's everywhere you cannot walk because in many ways we are all unclean.

Yes, I am fed up of walking alone hence I want and need to come off the path of God – Good God.

The road is too f***ing lonely and depressing.

I have no freedom because I cannot walk freely.

Yes the protection hence I am restricted. Cannot go to every land. Who the hell wants that?

I truly need freedom not slavery.

Yes, I feel like a slave with God hence I refuse many things and today I truly want to refuse God – Good God and do everything because I am way too lonely with him.

I need this freedom from the cage that I am in.
I need freedom to roam and be me. And as of late my feet are truly tied. As if I am to stay in this country.

There is nothing wrong with the country, I just don't want to be here nor live here. This is not my land that my spirit wants to be in hence it is a fight, a literal fight between my spirit and God – Good God. I know he sees what I cannot see and this is his way of protecting me, but he did not have to tie my feet. I need them to be loose not tied. I am not a shoelace. I need my feet.

Michelle
September 22, 2013

It's after 3 in the morning and I so feel defeated.

I can't sleep. I so want to be somewhere in Africa or the Caribbean at this hour in the morning.

Yes it would be just me because I so would not want someone or anyone disturbing my peace and tranquility.

I so want to be someplace different. I truly need to be in Africa but my feet are tied – bound. I cannot go anywhere – there.

Yes I am in a land where I so truly don't want to be in. I so truly don't like to watch TV and I don't. Only on rare occasions. If it was truly up to me, I wouldn't even have a TV. But because of the kids I have one. Not for me but for them.

Weird. I truly need to escape technology.

Need to escape emails, I phones and smart phones.

Man oh man bring back the dinosaur era. The dinosaur age where everything was slow paced and not so rushed – quiet.

No one was rushing here or rushing there.

No one invaded each other's land – space.

Now – a – days nothing is private including your pubic hair.

Humanity have and has gone wild because for the right price anyone can buy a skank.

Prostitutes are outdated. Skanks, whores and harlots are in hence they've replaced the prostitutes of old and modern day.

How low have we gone? How low have we sunk? Because the younger generation have gone wild. Buck wild. Hence there are no moral values when it comes to man – humans – humanity.

What a life? Oh well that's what we get when we kick goodness and good values to the curb – side. Our youngsters give the devil lab dances in their stinky videos. Hence the skanky dance – harlots of old.

We also get screwed up children living in a screwed up society. The devil's society that turns them into worse than whores, but money making machines that are jacked up on all sorts of drugs – chemicals, hairdos and devilish things.

Yes you can blame this on the parents also, because many work for vanity – the devil's pain.

Michelle and Michelle Jean September 22, 2013

Damn the 3:45 train.

No wonder we are sleep depraved.
Too much noise that bother our brain
Our restful sleep.

Man if there was a way to drown out the noise, I would drown it all out.

Who the hell can sleep if cars are on the road so late at nights.

Not to mention the loud ass motor cycles.

Wow. It's freaking amazing how everyone haven't gone crazy.

Freaking depressing.

Yes I can't sleep
Can't enjoy a restful sleep.

Need my life to be different.

I wonder if I lived atop the mountain top, if I would hear so much noise.

Yes I would. The airplane fly bys.

Damn I need a noise free environment, if not a reduced noise environment. Damn the noise.

Oh yea it's quiet down now.

Here come the snores – children snoring.

I need to snore like a banshee.

Oh wait I do that. I'm worse than an airplane hence the noise within the body.

I want to sleep but I can't sleep. My body is not tired. I am so wide awake.

No too cold for a walk and besides I am so not a night walker or stalker.

One day I will have a home gym. Yes, I would go get a good workout and tire myself out.

I so need a different life. I need something to tire myself out so that I can sleep at nights.

The fingers are getting tired from all this writing. You can see it in the flow of the ink – my writing.

Yes, I want to go back to bed but I cannot sleep. Oh well got to continue to write – writing.

Michelle
September 22, 2013

It's almost 4am and I so have to force myself back to sleep.

I have to go back to bed and sleep but can't will my body back to sleep. I have to force sleep and it is truly annoying.

I have to overload my brain with thoughts to truly fall back to sleep.

Yes not an easy feat when you wake up and can't go back to sleep.

Don't need a live blanket because after all these years, live blankets will not do. They will just annoy me.

Yes I am confused. Oh well that's just me. Sexual desires are rare to me.

Truly don't have a major list of someone that I would want to get with – do me.

I have a couple in mind but guess what they are gay. So scrap that, because a gay man is a gay man. Man this is so wrong but who cares. Certainly not me. I cannot sleep so anything goes. If I piss off anyone then so be it. I cannot sleep so therefore you cannot sleep. I am going to wake you up just to keep you up with me. My pain is your pain. My sleepless nights are your sleepless nights. If I have to go through this you have to go through it with me.

And no, I so do not need a sleeping aide to get me back to sleep.

And no, I so don't need a strong dick to put me back to sleep.

Maybe someone to rub my head.

No wait, he would be sleeping even snoring so scrap the rubbing of the head.

I want and need to go back to sleep but my body has too much energy.

Gotta force myself back to sleep.

My fingers are getting tired of writing. Hence I have to give them a break.

I so need to sleep. Oh well going back to bed and going to force myself to sleep.

Michelle
September 22, 2013

Yes the life is different and I so cannot stand this test because I know I am doing something wrong. I have to correct that wrong and get what I need to get done. Hence my feet are tied.

I know my pain hence I so want to run away from life.

No for real because I truly don't know if I am the only one to be going through this.

It's September 24, 2013 and Hold On by R. Kelly cannot get me going. I am still in this frustrated and stinking mood.

Dreams I so don't care about today because they truly do not make any sense to me. I am bound in hell and cannot get free.

I don't even want to think of God and all the goodness he's done for me. This is an ungrateful day and I cannot get over this freaking ungrateful mood as of late.

I know I am entitled to these days because everything cannot go straight this I know.

Today, I so want to cave without caring if it hurts God – Good God or not.

This is the way I feel and I have to get through this. I am no different from anyone – you.

I am human and I do have bad days. Worse than some yes but oh well this is just my hell.

I don't know why Good God has to bind my feet because this restriction makes you want to lash out severely at him and I've done this in this book.

Being one sucks because oneness is associated with pain and heartache.

Without God – Good God we do feel the pain and with him we feel the pain. This pain and suffering I do not like hence I so want to rebel but can't. I have no more strength and so don't want to listen anymore.

It's like I'm living wrong and everyone else is living right. Hence I doubt God – Good God and my life. He's shown me so many things but with all he's shown me, there is no true happiness for me.

You do his will, and at times you feel as if what you are doing is wrong. You doubt your sanity and what good is that?

This, books like these are my release and venting process at times.

You as a person see in words what I am going through. You often think I am crazy, need a shrink.

Don't worry I feel this way too.

This loneliness is beyond me. It's not like God – Good God cannot talk. He can but he does choose to alienate us – humans including his messengers.

<u>You see time, the clock and process of time but you are helpless to stop the destruction. You have to let death take its toll. You have to leave death alone and this is why death mask the truth. You cannot undo that which is done – ordained.</u>

Yes I see the darkness around me. I have the single key but getting to the mountain is one thing. Maybe I do not understand or overstand the scope of the mountain but I cannot change what I've seen. I cannot change the people that reside atop that mountain. I cannot add to that mountain because what I saw is what I told you.

Like I've said, God does not shut anyone out of his abode, we are the ones to shut ourselves out with our lies – sins.

My choice is my choice and it is not your choice. I have to come out of the darkness and move towards the light.

I have to make myself happy and in doing so, I have to comprehend and overstand the mountain.

I have the key but how do I use that key to open the door or doors that that mountain?

I have to know the full truth and if God – Good God is not giving me the full truth, then he too is wrong. And if he is wrong then I am wrong and what you are reading is wrong therefore, making you wrong also.

I know the mountain but getting to the mountain is another story. Hence I am tired of bugging God for everything.

Tired of being the odd one out that must battle to stay alive. Not just in the spiritual but in the physical realm as well.

Now you know my frustration and I do hope you understand and overstand what I am going through.

__Know that the chosen of God – Good God cannot fail or fall. I see my fall hence I go to God – Good God with my pain. I fear not man – humanity because evil must do what it must do to stay alive and keep alive.__

I worry not about what evil do and does because evil hath not life. Evil hath a time and his time is up 1313, which I equate and say is December 2013.

Evil nations must fall.
Evil empires must crumble.
Evil people must go to hell and die.

__The devil's secret society which is under the order of Melchesidec must crumble – fall infinitely down. They will never rise again, hence shortly many billionaires will lose it all. The Abrahamic Code of Death – Animal and Human sacrifices is done.__

__The 24 000 years of sin is done hence your 4 and twenty elders in the book of sin. Each elder had one thousand (1 000) years to manipulate and deceive humanity. Hence your 24 princes – demons. Your army time – time of war. This time war time was allotted to the White race because they are the fighters on the planet earth but yet know not what they are fighting for.__

Death must fight – kill to get going hence the skin of the white race represents spiritual death and the skin of the black race represents physical death.

Spiritual death is the deadlier of the two. White Death is superior to Black Death because White Death is final death and everyone must become white in death. No one can become black in death they must become white. This is the way it is hence your final judgement – death of life. Meaning death of your spirit.

Goodness is represented by darkness – black energy and not colour of skin. Darkness surrounds me I've told you this. This darkness I cannot see in. I have to feel my way through. My eyes have to become clear and clean in order for me to see in this darkness. I have the key. One single key in my hand and trust me I am so going to use that key come what may.

Michelle Jean
September 24, 2013

It's shaping up to be a trying month for me but I truly don't care.

I truly don't care what happens now in my life because all I've tried has failed.

I am so fed up of failure that I so want to walk away from all.

In all that I write I am fed up because God – Good God has and have failed me.

I don't give a shit about anything anymore because I know the spirit and soul is gone.

I want and need it to go because I cannot stand anything anyone around me anymore.

Don't care about the mess I live in. Fuck everything because the more you clean is the more your fucking kids make a mess.

The more you talk is the more they don't fucking listen.

Fuck everything now. I truly give up because my fucking life is fucked up.

Jacked up by God and man.

I truly want and need to leave the physical and spiritual behind because both worlds are lies – a fucking mess.

If God – Good God cannot fix the spiritual, how the hell can he fix the physical including fixing man?

God – Good God is a fucking mess.

Death and sin is a fucking mess. Hence you are a fucking mess.

Trust me, I need an undo button for both worlds because both worlds fuck up your life royally. Neither world are on the same accord. There's no unity in both worlds.

Why the fuck should anyone commit themselves to either. There is not happiness in either world.

Fuck. God's gone. So why the fuck should humanity try to find him or reach him?

What purpose does he serve?

What does he profit man – humanity if he can't truly help you?

Yes he's real but today I am at my wits end. I am fucking stressed and in need of a fucking vacation. Yes darkness surrounds me because I see the mountain from the darkness but is it truly the mountain I see or is it me? Am I that darkness?

Is it truly God – Good God leading me or some black demon that is trying to take me to hell with him?

In all that we do we say God but is it truly God?

Yes confusion sets in hence I am so in the dark when it comes to the mountain and finding the mountain.

Tell me something. If God truly loved us so, would he continue to be so far away?

Would he not be united with us in every way? Would he not be there for us in our stressful days? ***No scrap this one because he is there with us in our stressful days and ways. Hence I vent to him in this way.***

Yes I will forever cast doubt because like I said, I am in the dark when it comes to him and I so do not want to be in the dark anymore.

Michelle and Michelle Jean
September 25, 2013

Yes I've lost a fucking screw because my life is fucked up with God.

Yes I'm fucking insane
Fucking stressed out
Fucking tired

Yes fucking tired of talking to a silent and fucking dead god.

What fucking life does he have if I am stressed out because of him and all the bullshit in my life? Bullshit that surrounds me.

He can't even take me on a fucking BC vacation!!

Yes I am stressed to the max hence today fuck everything.

I need a fucking loony bin.
A fucking universe void of stress and pain.
A fucking universe void of God and his fucking bullshit stress and mess.

Yes stress has a hold of me and I so don't care if I sin royally.

This I truly blame God for because he knows my need and refuses to help me. So on this day, I truly don't give a fuck about sin and respect.

Why the fuck should I continue to give my truth and true love in vain? Yes to a god that is truly not there.

I am wasting my precious time. Precious time that I could be spending doing something else.

Yes I am truly fed up of God because he's only there when he chooses to be.

Look at my stress and pain and truly tell me, if God is truly there for me, when it comes to heartache and pain and my true happiness.

No for real people. Truly look back and read all these books and tell me if I've not complained constantly about happiness when it come to God – Good God?

So, if the god you truly love can't truly make you happy, why the fuck am I holding on to him?

Why the fuck am I wasting my precious time on someone – a god that truly don't give a fuck about me and my happiness?

Michelle Jean
September 25, 2013

Yes people you can call me ungrateful because I so want and need to be.

I so need to be ungrateful

My kids are fucking nasty
They are fucking noisy

I am all out fucked because I want to run away from my kids and never come back.

What possessed me to have them anyway? Don't answer that.

Shhh, don't.

And no the sex was not that fucking nice at least for one anyway. Well both.

Yes silence is golden to me but this month is turning out to be a fucked up month.

I am fucking tired of the noise including noisy keyboards.

Tired of the friends that come over with di bag a nise.

Yes I want to snap rude.

Yes my spirit snapped rude today hence I saw the dark blue and blackness of my spiritual eye – soul.

Yes I saw the evil of my spiritual eye – soul and people it is not pretty. It is damned ugly.

How do I describe it?

You know those people that tattoo their eyeballs? Well that's how my spiritual eye – soul looked. That dark and ugly.

When it snapped rude, I saw dark blue first then I saw the ugliness of my spiritual eye – soul.

Yes I sinned rude people and now I know the ugliness of my sins. Wow.

So because I saw the ugliness of my spiritual anger – sin, I know now to tattoo your eyeballs is an ultimate sin. Yes a spiritual sin.

The tattooing of the eyeballs is what our sins look like in its pure state of ugliness.

Yes darkness is around me and I've seen this darkness. This darkness I cannot see in. It's as if I am being blinded.

As if I am blind because I know I cannot see.

But to the way I feel now. I truly don't care. I need my spirit to snap. I need it to vent the way it needs to vent.

Like I said, I feel trapped. As if I am bound and I refuse to let God – Good God tie me – my feet.

I refuse to be tied down by God and man hence my spirit seeks escape. It needs to escape and I am bound. Why I truly do not know. All I know is our flesh is the true prison – cage for our spirit or soul.

My spirit wants and need to escape this prison and I cannot find the right outlet to flee from this forsaken world I am trapped in.

I am not a slave hence he God – Good God must know about true love. True love should not be painful.

True love should not bound or bind. But yet with him Good God, I am feeling pain. I am going through pain.

I don't know but maybe this is the lesson that I need to teach.

Maybe this is what God wants me to tell you. We of ourselves are the ones to be in the dark. The mountain is there and it is us that must open our eyes and come out of the dark and move towards that mountain – him.

Maybe he wanted me to teach you and tell you about what spiritual evil looks like. These spiritual evils are our sins hence making our spirit that dark and ugly.

This is why I tell you our sins await us in hell and when we see them, they are going to be ugly to look upon.

Many of us will cry and we do cry when we see them because we will be seeing self – the ugliness of within. The ugliness of the sins we commit and do on a daily basis.

And yes I comprehend the venting because if my spirit did not vent in this way, I would not be able to tell you or show you what our sins look like in the spiritual realm.

Michelle Jean
September 25, 2013

I need to run away from my life.
I need to run away from everything.

Life is too painful
Stressed

Why did we have to choose a life of sin and pain?

Why the fuck did I have to be a single mother?

This bullshit is a sin.
Single motherhood is a fucking curse because all the work is on you the mother alone.

Most of these scumbags that leave raising their children on the woman alone should be hung by their dicks and at death their fucking dicks should be fucking cut off and stuffed down their whoring and deceiving throats.

Yes I am in pain because I am the one stressed out – hurting.

Yes other women are feeling the pain. Some worse than me but who feels it knows it.

To me, God only cares about these fucking sperm donors that care nothing for their children.

To me, he God preserves them; don't even fucking chastise them for not taking care of their children. Hence women were to have pain in child birth.

Yes Genesis was just fucking telling the sperm donors – cock******* what to do. Telling them to leave the woman and let them raise the children alone hence leaving her/us in pain. Leaving her to suffer and die a painful death.

To me, he God upholds nastiness and slackness when it comes to morals and values – the family unit.

It's fucking immoral for one parent to raise a child – children alone.

It's fucking immoral for a man or woman to abandon their children because the father or mother is not there to help – raise them. (Adoption and adopted parents excluded).

Yes, I am pissed but like I said, as a single parent raising children on her own. Who feels it knows it.

Michelle Jean
September 25, 2013

Yes this is my fall and I so don't give a fuck if God walks away from me.

I truly want him to.
Need him to because I am so not happy with him.

Yes I have to honour my word and because I live by my word – truth, I cannot abandon his ass no matter how I vent and take my frustrations out on him.

Yes the doubt will be there but until he takes me out of my fucking mess, I will continue to be a fucking hot mess. And yes I am trying on my own if you truly want to know.

Yes I sinned reckless and rude September 25, 2013 because I smelt the fire burning. Meaning the cigarette burning but I don't care. I don't give a fuck if the agents and demons of hell were in my room.

They too, death and hell can truly fuck the hell off.

Who the BC cares about fucking death and hell.

To the way I feel, I so want death and hell to challenge me so I can beat the fuck out them and release some of my pent up anger and stress – rage.

Trust me, if I could rearrange the face of sin and death including hell by beating the crap out of them worse than a boxer and a MMA fighter rolled up in one, trust me I would. I would so not hesitate because death and hell including the demons of hell would burn down. Not even ash would be left of them when I am through.

I need a release hence I am writing this book.

I am trying to release but can't. I so want to do something stupid but what?

Yes the spirit – my light within is a different hue. Of pinkish blue but who the fuck cares? September is my month to vent well at least the Libra is out. Virgo is so gone what a pity. Now Libra has stepped in and I so want her to go. Yes, this is my anger time and trust me it is pent up and so coming out.

Yes, the volcano is erupting and I so pity those who fucking stand in my way.

Yes, I want to mow down and fucking destroy. And if the devil comes in my way, I will fucking destroy him without hesitation.

Michelle and Michelle Jean
September 25, 2013

No I am so not done
I need a psyche ward so I can have me some fun

Yes I am gone
I need psychological help

Hell no.
Fuck that. I just need a fucking vacation so that I can be happy and get away from my nasty kids dem.

Yes I need to do me
I need to break away from God – Good God
I need to be free

Need to do something for me

I need to release myself from God – Good God

Need to truly be alone
Need to get away from the noise because it's getting to me.

And yes I did talk to the fucking kids about the noise but it's as if they don't care.

I am tired. Hence soon I am going to fucking walk away from them and truly disinherit them.

Michelle Jean
September 25, 2013

Yes the spirit is gone
Mad as fuck

Yes I am getting to despise and hate my life

You know what fuck all of this
Why the hell am I letting God hold me back?

I don't hold him back. So why the fuck should I
make him or allow him to dictate my life.

I cannot dictate his.
He doesn't listen to me. So fuck it all. I am going
to Jamaica. Clean or unclean I am so going.

All of earth – the lands and people of the earth
are fucking unclean anyway. God is not here on
earth and who the fuck cares about the spiritual
realm anyway? I need to be happy hence God –
Good God does not make me truly happy or
happy.

Michelle and Michelle Jean
September 25, 2013

Yes my life is fucked and this is why I tell all of you that I will never convert anyone. And besides no one can be converted anyway.

Yes my life is hell and despite me choosing life – the goodness of life, my life is not easy. I have bad days. More bad days than I want.

I don't know if this is what I am to teach you because like I said, I am in the dark when it comes to the mountain. I see the mountain but reaching it is and has always been a problem.

This is why I tell God – Good God that I refuse to tell anyone to choose or chose him. Good life is good but I refuse to tell anyone now to choose him because I truly do not find happiness in him.

As individuals we must live by our truths and goodness. Our good and true word.

In my quest for happiness and truth, I cannot find it in the god that I have chosen. Maybe over time I will but not now.

I am going through the pain right now and it's not easy. **_Yes it's hard on earth. So can you imagine what this pain is like in hell?_**

People – Family, I don't know if I need God – Good God to be what he truly cannot be or if I am just screwed up in the brain like the rest of humanity?

I know the pathway of truth is not easy and sometimes we fall off like me in this book and so many others.

It's not to say that I don't truly love God – Good God but he must also know our hurt and pain. He God – Good God must see with us. Both realms (the physical and spiritual) are not on the same accord and if they are not on the same accord then both realms are a lie and we will never be on the same accord with God – Good God.

United both realms should be but they are not. Both realms are divided hence we fall and this is why I am falling and have fallen.

One cannot be in the east and the other in the north.

I know good and evil cannot be united because one is clean whilst the other is unclean. What I need as a person and as a child of Good God is true unity between me and him.

If there is no unity then we cannot come together and all that is he showing me is a lie. Yes many things have and has come true but what about me? What about my happiness – the things that makes me happy?

<u>Like I've said, God cannot say he loves us so and continue to see us hurt – suffer. That is not true love it is hate.</u>

His word – the word of God means something but if he God – Good God cannot honour his word then he too has become a liar just like Satan – evil. And yes he too must die because he gave us false hope and led us to our deaths.

<u>He God – Good God must be united with us and if he's not then he is a liar. True love is not about the individual it's about all.</u>

Yes I can truly love me, but what about the good people that surrounds me? I know evil can only love evil hence evil hath a greater pull over good but that should not be.

<u>If God – Good God truly loved then evil would not pull good or suck on to good. He Good God would make us repel evil so that we don't have days like mine as outlined in my venting in this book.</u>

Hence I will forever say I will not convert anyone or tell anyone to choose or chose my god because I know the hell hole of a road that I have to walk on.

I know the hell hole of a road humanity has to walk and face and it's not pretty.

My god does not listen hence it takes him years upon years to hear me and he does ignore me. So to say choose my god, no. If your god is working for you then keep him because he is your god and yes this is why there are many gods for many different thing.

I cannot knowingly tell you to choose pain and suffering. See my hardships and learn. Like I said, the spiritual and physical realm is not united hence we cannot be united with God – Good God. Our lives will continue to be a lie. God – Good God must now unite us so that we are not so confused and stressed out over him – life like me.

He Good God have to do better in securing good life – us as humans.

And yes this is where hell and heaven is separated. The separation of water. Hence water separates good from all evil in both realms.

And yes not everyone suffers. You don't have to suffer if you choose wisely.

Like I said, maybe what I am looking for in God – Good God he is not capable of giving it to me. No one can.

Maybe what I want and need him Good God to be he cannot be hence I am the one in the dark.

*I am the one that must find the light like I said. I am the one that must now wash myself clean yet again because you **NOW KNOW WHAT OUR SINS LOOK LIKE IN THE SPIRITUAL REALM.***

I can no longer sin.

Hence this morning I am somewhat free. Hence I played No Weapon by Fred Hammond and Take Me to the King by Tamela Mann.

I know no weapon formed against God – Good God can or will prosper. Hence this book is like a weapon when it comes to him.

In a way I need it to be because I need him to get me. Truly feel my pain and anguish. Yes we all have dark days hence this book.

At times we need rescuing but for me I have to rescue myself. And I hate rescuing myself. Yes I know he is there with me holding my hand, but why can't God – Good God be that one good human that I need in the physical realm?

And yes maybe that's it. I want and need him to be human. Something he cannot be.

I know the cleanliness of him hence mess drives me crazy. I do hate and despise a messy place – home.

One person cannot do all the work hence we snap, are stressed. This is what I am trying to tell the kids but they cannot get it and I so can't wait until they have children for them to get it. They will feel the pain worse than me.

And yes I've always cherished neatness. It's now that I have kids that I cannot keep up. My house has and have been messy. Trust me the nasty men and women you associate with and lay with cause your life to become messy and disorderly. And yes your place cannot stay clean hence God – Good God cannot come in.

So on this day, September 26, 2013 Good God I ask your forgiveness for snapping so rude. I needed the spirit to vent rude and it did hence I know what our sins look like.

I literally saw my sins with my eyes because it was before me – in front of me. Now humanity truly knows what their sin look like.

It is that dark and ugly hence the tattoo of the eyeballs. The tattoos of sin literally in the physical and spiritual realm.

God, Good God, our sins are that ugly?

Wow. Now I am seeing everything. So truly forgive me because I so needed this book. I so needed to go ham on you.

I had to take my spiritual frustrations out on you. I had to see me – my sins and you did show them to me.

So now, as I continue to come to you will my physical and spiritual frustrations, truly thank you for being you. Truly thank you for listening to me and taking on my pain, that which truly hurts me and ails me.

Michelle Jean
September 26, 2013